THIS WALKER BOOK BELONGS TO:

_____

_____

_____

_____

First published individually as
Bend and Stretch, *Making Friends*,
Mum's Home and *This Little Nose*
in 1987 by Walker Books Ltd
87 Vauxhall Walk, London SE11 5HJ

This edition published 1998

10 9 8 7 6 5 4 3 2

This book has been typeset in Bembo Educational.

Printed in Hong Kong/China

British Library Cataloguing in Publication Data
A catalogue record for this book is
available from the British Library.

ISBN 0-7445-6010-1

MUM AND ME

JAN ORMEROD

WALKER BOOKS
AND SUBSIDIARIES
LONDON • BOSTON • SYDNEY

Contents

Shopping

Mum's home.
What's in her basket?

Things for a baby.

Basket

And what else?

7

Dig deep.

Blow Mum's nose.
Have a banana ...

and a snooze.

Making

Playing with pieces of cloth.

Resting on a pillow.

Friends

Playing with

reels of thread.

Playing with buttons.

13

Playing with wool.

Sitting together.

14

Making friends
with someone new.

Cuddling.

This Little

This little nose
   is red and runny.

This little nose
   is a very little nose.

This little nose
   is a long nose.

Nose

Who's a nosy,
furry fellow?

Two little noses
close together.

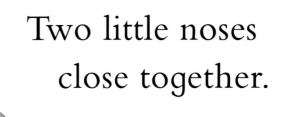

You'll feel better
in the morning.

Bend and

Breathe
  in and up.

Left leg, right leg,
  round and round.

18

Stretch

Breathe out
and down.

Stretching
that way.

Stretching
this way.

Tickle, tickle, tickle.
Giggle, giggle, giggle.

In, out, up, down,
round and round.